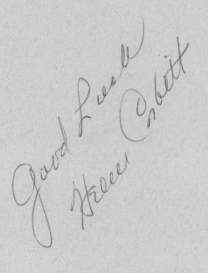

W9-BWU-149

Good Luck
Helen Corbitt

Helen Corbitt
Cooks
for Looks

Also by Helen Corbitt

Helen Corbitt's Cookbook
Helen Corbitt's Potluck

Helen Corbitt Cooks for Looks

An Adventure
In Low-Calorie Eating

by
HELEN CORBITT

Director of Restaurants
at Neiman-Marcus

HOUGHTON MIFFLIN COMPANY

BOSTON

Decorations by Dorothy Michaelson

Fifth Printing w

Copyright © 1967 by Helen Corbitt
All rights reserved including the right to reproduce
this book or parts thereof in any form
Library of Congress Catalog Card Number: 67-29415
Printed in the United States of America

To Stanley Marcus

PREFACE

WHEN I was asked to plan and execute low-calorie meals for a luxury health spa, I asked myself, "What do you want to get started in that kind of thing for?" I am noted for good things to eat, cooked with all the ingredients that make eating an enjoyable pastime. About the same time my doctor told me to lose weight, so I went to work at cutting down, but I still enjoy eating.

Calories are not something you can harness. You cannot see them, hear them, smell them or feel them, but you can certainly see the results of too many of them.

Most diets boil down to lean meat, cottage cheese and eggs, and you cannot do much to make these attractive. I am concerned with how food is presented, and being a former hospital dietitian, I am interested in balance, both nutritional and decorative. I believe you can lose weight, stay healthy, and enjoy your food with this kind of thinking. I hope you will agree with me as you try this collection of lower-in-calorie menus and recipes.

HELEN CORBITT

CONTENTS

Helen Corbitt
Cooks
for Looks

1

GENERAL
ADVICE

Americans are blessed, or cursed, depending on how
you look at it, with a disease of the salivary glands.
We eat too much! It is easy to cure: merely cut down
on your calorie intake; it is as simple as that. Without
getting too involved with a word much publicized today,
we can say that a calorie is a unit of heat. You need
this heat to live, as an automobile needs gasoline to
run, but if you consume more calories than you need,
you store them, and if you store too many, you become
overweight.

Then you go on a diet — your health demands it;
now and then fashion decrees it. Whatever the reason,
if you are on a diet you have to stick with it. If you

are inclined to obesity, then you learn to say "no" most of your life.

There is no such thing as an epicurean meal with heavy indulgence in all things good to eat. Webster defines an epicure as one given to dainty indulgence in the pleasures of the table. Perhaps "dainty" is a good word to adopt; be dainty in your eating habits and not a ravenous wolf.

For you who love good food, cutting down the amount you normally eat needs a new approach to an old habit, and bewailing your lot in life doesn't help one bit. However, the enjoyment you gain from discussing your diet with whoever will listen is part of the game. You will find lots of listeners today; everyone is talking about diets, all kinds, good and not so good.

From my viewpoint — and I eat too much too, both professionally where I taste too heavily, and socially because I enjoy it — it is both difficult and ridiculous to make life more complicated by preparing exotic low-calorie casseroles and desserts that may look glorious, but do not taste so. Why not go into an adventure in good eating as simply and naturally as possible? Try the flavor of food without added butter and excessive cream, without sugar and "char." Use more fruits and vegetables in the natural state, broil and roast meat instead of frying; you will be amazed how soon you will not like the flavor of burned fat. Use natural seasonings, like grated peel of citrus fruits, herbs both fresh and dried. There are endless ways — just look for them with your mind and eye and taste buds.

Change the look of things with something as simple as serving tomato juice in a stemmed crystal wine glass with a cucumber stick to stir it — it will taste better. Use watercress and parsley and even celery leaves (you usually throw them away) in profusion to decorate. You don't have to eat them (who cares?), but a full plate makes you think you have more and

2

looks better. When I was a young dietitian at Cornell Medical Center in New York City, I remember talking to a patient who was difficult — so unlike me! — and refused to discuss her diet, but her parting shot at me as I left the room, "For heaven's sake, make it attractive," made a lasting impression on me.

These menus and recipes are merely guides to a lower-in-calorie regime that I think will help you psychologically, physically and morale-wise, and not throw you into the frantic low-calorie jitters. They are planned with your family in mind. There is no reason for you to be set apart from the rest. Just add more for them. Don't be too different with a routine that is frustrating, and don't be a martyr. Remember this: the world will look brighter as you slim. You will feel better too.

The menus are designed with an idea of balance, and are full of vitamins and minerals, but low on carbohydrates and fats. They have been tried out at The Greenhouse in Arlington, Texas, a new luxury health spa for women, owned and operated by the Great Southwest Corporation of Texas, and guided by Charles of the Ritz and Neiman-Marcus of Dallas.

The amounts are planned for 850 calories a day. At The Greenhouse the usual weight loss is from five to seven pounds a week, with a planned routine of exercise and massage. Some results are fantastic, some mediocre, but the individual has to be taken into consideration. Younger people lose more quickly than older, as a rule, and if you cheat with a chocolate bar each day or too many highballs, you will not lose as fast as if you don't.

These are some of the do's I recommend for a diet routine:

1. Use sugar substitutes. I doubt if one is better than another, but people have different reactions to food,

1 3-ounce beef patty
1 5-ounce steak, no fat
1 scoop diet ice cream or ice, that you make yourself
1 generous ½ cup whip, snow pudding, gelatin
  dessert
Tea and coffee, limited at mealtimes

You may cook with wine, beer and cognac, but you must be sure to cook with it. Heat evaporates the alcohol and you have only the flavor left, which makes food more interesting.

The awful, awful truth is that

1 glass still wine	contains about	75 calories
1 glass champagne		100 calories
1 martini		125 calories
1 plain whiskey or gin		75 calories
a limeade or lemonade (the kind you order at a soda counter)		100 calories
Coca-Cola		60 calories
a glass of beer		100 calories
an after-dinner liqueur		75 calories per ounce
a piece of most 2-crust pies		400 calories
a chocolate bar		300 calories
Fudge Love		heaven only knows!
Zodiac Ice Cream Pie		750 calories
a piece of iced cake		400 calories
a French pastry, average size		250 calories
a Danish pastry		300 calories
a Club sandwich		600 calories
a nice juicy sirloin steak		500 calories
ham and 1 egg		450 calories

These are some of the easy-to-find low-calorie foods:

Vegetables, raw or plainly cooked, no sauce or butter: asparagus, artichokes, bamboo shoots, bean sprouts, hearts of palm and snow peas, broccoli, Brussels sprouts, cabbage and Chinese cabbage, capers, cauliflower, carrots, celery and cucumbers. All salad greens, mushrooms, morilles and scallions, radishes, sauerkraut, green beans, spinach, zucchini, patty pan and yellow squash, tomatoes, turnips and truffles.

Fresh fruits: grapefruit, oranges and tangerines, melons, berries, apples, apricots, peaches, pineapple and papaya, lemons and limes and cherries (also water-packed canned fruits).

Fish: white-meated fish and shellfish, plainly cooked with no sauce or butter. Water- or brine-packed tunafish.

Soups: only clear bouillon, chicken, beef, tomato or turtle.

Eggs, especially the whites, and — hooray! — caviar.

Lean meats (lamb and veal have fewer calories than beef); chicken and white meat of turkey, quail and pheasant, doves (not fried).

Skim milk, buttermilk made from skim milk, cottage cheese without added cream and made from skim milk.

Coffee and tea with no sugar or cream.

These are some high-calorie foods:

Jams, jellies and marmalades, canned fruits in syrups.

Nuts, all kinds. There are no low-calorie nuts, regardless of the ads.

Bottled and canned juices, unless otherwise designated on the label.

Potatoes, both white and sweet, potato chips, lima and butter beans, Hubbard squash, peas and corn, dried peas and beans, black-eyed peas, garbanzos and lentils.

Cream and butter, sour cream and mayonnaise, ice cream, sherbet, and all things made with them.

All fried foods, all breads, muffins, biscuits, pancakes, crackers, pies and pastries, cake and candy. Peanut butter, guava paste, pâté de foie gras.

You should learn and remember quantities for the diet regime. Adopt the idea of eating average-sized helpings — no extra-large and no second helpings.

Let's take a sample menu for one day:

Breakfast

1/2 grapefruit
1 slice melba toast
2 cups black coffee or tea

Midmorning

1 cup vegetable broth or bouillon

Lunch

1/2 cold boiled Maine lobster, 1 1/2 pound
Shredded cucumbers and capers, to fill the tomalley
    cavity (all you wish)
Spinach salad mimosa:
    1 cup spinach leaves
    1/2 hard-cooked egg white, chopped
    2 teaspoons wine vinegar and oil dressing
Black coffee or tea

Midafternoon

Hot tea with lemon

Dinner

Cold consommé served on the rocks in a small
  wine glass
2 or 3 pickled shrimp
$^1/_2$ broiled squab chicken — 1 pound
2 tablespoons slivered green beans
1 braised celery heart
1 cup green salad with $^1/_2$ tomato and
1 teaspoon Zesty Dressing
1 tablespoon puréed strawberries over
$^1/_2$ cup baked custard
Black coffee or tea

FIRST
VVEEK

If you are slimming, start with cutting down at breakfast. A half grapefruit, or a sliced orange, or your favorite fruit, fresh or freshly cooked without added sugar. Black coffee — you will enjoy it more without sugar or cream — or tea. A slice of melba toast, if you must, but make it yourself, and if you think the world looks too dismal, an egg poached or boiled (leave the yolk in the dish).

Hot tea or coffee between meals is permissible, and a cup of hot vegetable broth midmorning will make the world look brighter; it is filled with vitamins, especially potassium.

VEGETABLE BROTH

1 carrot, washed not peeled
12 fresh green beans or pea pods
Some mushroom stems if you have them
2 stalks celery
3 small yellow squash, unpeeled
1 onion
A handful of spinach or watercress or parsley

Cover vegetables with water and simmer until they are soft. Strain, season with artificial salt. This is merely an outline. Use any vegetable, including the skins of potatoes. It is good for everyone!

In the middle of the afternoon, if you need an added push and crave some flavor to it, fresh fruit of any kind, put into a blender with cracked ice, makes a delightful pick-me-up. Use it for the before-dinner cocktail too. I like to take a few pieces of fresh pineapple, perhaps a few strawberries, a small piece of melon, any fruit as long as it is fresh (about 1 cup altogether), add a couple of ice cubes, a sprig of mint if I have it, and put them all in the blender until they form a mush. Not many calories, but so refreshing.

The great American public who work eat lunch out. Unless you have an eat-at-home family, or some of your neighbors come in, lunch may be a bore for you, but eat it you must.

Here goes: four weeks of menus. Switch them around if you like, substitute similar items, but try them!

FIRST DAY

Lunch

1/4 broiled chicken, rubbed with lemon juice before
broiling

Asparagus with grated orange peel
Cinnamon broiled grapefruit

Dinner

Jellied madrilène (buy it in cans). Serve in shallow
crystal bowls or compotes with lump crabmeat
and capers in the center. It is a beautiful low-
calorie sight to sit down to. A twist of lemon
for you. Pass sour cream for those who do
not care.

Broiled flank steak, lightly rubbed with brown
mustard before cooking. (Use your finger tips!
Encased in wax paper if you are squeamish.)

Fresh green beans, cut slanty-eyed, sprinkled with
dill

Lemon ice packed in orange shells

SECOND DAY

A Bridge Luncheon

Perhaps a demitasse of hot chicken broth
Half of fresh pineapple, scooped out and filled
with orange and grapefruit sections, slivers of
cold chicken on top
Pass a bowl of yogurt dressing

Dinner

Chilled canned celery-heart salad sprinkled with
finely chopped hard-cooked egg white and
parsley

Wine vinegar and vegetable oil dressing

A thick broiled lamb chop, all the fat cut off for
you

Fresh spinach soufflé

A baked half of tomato sprinkled with orégano
and Parmesan cheese

Fresh pears poached in red wine

THIRD DAY

Lunch

Cold boiled lobster tail with a jellied cucumber salad and yogurt remoulade

Dinner

Gazpacho (a demitasse before dinner in the living room)

Thin slices of boiled lean beef. (I like to use a butt, top or bottom, and serve with the juices.)

Fresh little white onions cooked in the beef broth

Fresh cabbage quarters, cooked covered 10 minutes in boiling water

A few peas and chopped parsley to sprinkle over

Marinated beets

Stewed apples and mandarin oranges

FOURTH DAY

Lunch

A cheese custard
Fresh spinach and mushroom salad

Dinner with Close Friends

A tray of nibbles before dinner: raw carrot sticks, thin slices of raw white turnips and zucchini, cherry tomatoes and cucumber fingers, all icy cold and crisp (and you can eat all you like)

Broiled whole squab chicken

Pink applesauce, flavored with horseradish (make it pink with vegetable coloring or beet juice)

Mushroom soufflé

Broccoli Piquante

Pots de Crème

FIFTH DAY

Lunch

Bowl of hot tomato bouillon
Sliced egg and canned artichoke salad bowl with
  wine vinegar dressing
Fingers of fresh pineapple

Dinner

Yogurt soup (serve in crystal again over a green
  leaf from the yard)
Oven-baked fresh salmon steak
Swedish cucumbers
A bouquet of vegetables on a silver tray: baby
  beets with capers, fresh okra, little patty pan
  or white squash with lemon mint sauce
Grapefruit sections with puréed strawberries to
  spoon over

SIXTH DAY

Lunch (*no doubt there is a man about the house*)

Broiled beef patty
Baked half of tomato piled high with spinach purée
Hot German cole slaw

Dinner (*A kitchen buffet*)

Tiñola (boiled chicken with vegetables). Serve
  from the pot you cook it in.
Relish salad bowl
A freezer of Three Fruit Sherbet

SUNDAY

Dinner (noonish)

Jellied spring salad
Roasted turkey breast Singapore
Fresh green beans, okra and onion rings tossed
and sprinkled with coconut
Carrot pudding
Warm English custard over very cold canned
apricots

Sunday Night

Hot claret consommé (you buy it)
Slices of ripe cantaloupe, thin slice of Swiss cheese
and cold meat. (You can buy lean, very thin
slices of corned beef in packages, and this goes
well with the melon and cheese.)

THE RECIPES YOU NEED

CINNAMON BROILED GRAPEFRUIT

Grapefruit, hot or cold, is a nice way to begin or end
a meal. Sprinkle a little cinnamon over the sectioned
half and bake in a 300° oven for 10 minutes. Remove
and run under broiler to brown or leave it in the oven
until the edges are brown and the sections puffed.

CHICKEN BROTH

1 3-to-4-pound hen
1 stalk celery
Few sprigs parsley
1 small onion
1 small carrot
Water to cover

Put in a deep kettle and simmer for several hours or 15

until chicken is tender. You may add bay leaf, a sprig of thyme, 3 whole cloves stuck in the onion for added flavor. Remove hen, strain and set aside to cool. The fat will come to the top. Refrigerate to solidify. Remove fat and reheat to serve hot. Season to your taste. Add gelatin for a jellied soup, 1 teaspoon for each cup of broth. If you wish a clearer broth after you remove the hen and strain, break 2 eggs into the pot, shell and all. Bring to a fast boil. Set aside until egg floats on top, then strain again through a very fine sieve or through cheese cloth.

YOGURT DRESSING

2 egg yolks, hard-cooked and pressed through sieve
2 raw egg yolks
1 teaspoon dry mustard
2 cups yogurt
2 teaspoons lemon juice
salt substitute

Add raw egg yolks to cooked egg yolks with the mustard. Beat in rest of ingredients slowly. Keep refrigerated.

WINE VINEGAR DRESSING

$1/2$ cup red wine vinegar
2 tablespoons vegetable salad oil
$1/2$ clove garlic crushed
1 tablespoon chopped parsley
pinch of oregano or tarragon

Put in a bottle and shake well. Sprinkle sparingly over salads or cooked vegetables in place of butter.

GAZPACHO
(For four)

2 large peeled ripe tomatoes
1/4 cucumber peeled
2 tablespoons chopped green pepper
2 tablespoons vegetable salad oil
1 tablespoon wine vinegar
1 cup tomato juice
1 teaspoon grated onion
fresh ground pepper
salt substitute

Chop tomatoes, cucumbers and green peppers to a fine mush. Add rest of ingredients and chill. Or put everything in an electric blender. I like it better chopped by hand. Serve in very cold demitasse cups before dinner in the living room, or as a first course in tomato cups with an ice cube in the center, or in your two-handled cream soup cups — any way you choose. The tomato cups are made by choosing firm tomatoes, cutting off the blossom end and carefully scraping out the insides. Quite a beautiful way to serve it. This is a good pick-me-up too, when things look mighty grim.

TOMATO BOUILLON
(For four or six)

1/4 cup diced celery
1/4 cup diced carrots
1/4 cup diced onion
few sprigs of parsley
4 cups tomato juice
1/2 teaspoon white pepper
6 whole cloves
1 bay leaf
1/8 teaspoon thyme
2 cups hot consommé, chicken or beef

Simmer celery, carrots, onions, parsley, tomato juice

and seasonings covered for 1 hour. Strain, add hot consommé, and reheat. Season to your taste.

YOGURT SOUP

$1/4$ cup raisins
3 cups yogurt
$1/4$ cup skim milk
1 hard-cooked egg
6 ice cubes
$1/4$ cup finely diced cucumber
2 tablespoons finely chopped green onion
1 cup cold water
1 tablespoon chopped parsley
1 teaspoon dill weed

Soak raisins in cold water till puffed. Put yogurt in mixing bowl with skim milk, chopped egg, ice cubes, cucumber and onion. Stir well. Add raisins and water they soaked in. Refrigerate. Serve with chopped parsley and dill. Nice, too, to serve at a cocktail party for non-drinkers!

SPINACH SOUFFLÉ
(For six)

1 cup well drained, finely chopped raw spinach (a blender is best for this)
2 tablespoons whipped margarine
3 tablespoons flour
1 cup skim milk
5 egg yolks
5 egg whites
$1/4$ teaspoon white pepper
$1/2$ teaspoon salt substitute

Melt margarine, add flour. Cook until bubbly. Add milk and cook until thickened. Add spinach. Cook over hot water for 30 minutes. Cool slightly. Add egg yolks. Cool till cold, fold in stiffly beaten egg whites.

Rub a 3-quart soufflé dish with a little margarine and pour in mixture. Bake at 375° for 30 minutes.

MUSHROOM SOUFFLÉ
(For four or six)

1 pound fresh mushrooms
1 small onion, finely diced
4 tablespoons whipped margarine
2 tablespoons flour
$3/4$ cup chicken broth or skim milk
4 egg yolks
4 egg whites
$1/2$ teaspoon salt substitute
$1/4$ cup grated Parmesan cheese

Wash, dry, and detach stems, but do not peel. Chop stems and sauté with the onion in 1 tablespoon of the margarine. Make a cream sauce by melting the 2 tablespoons of the margarine, add the flour. Cook until bubbly, add chicken broth or skim milk. Cook until thickened. Add sautéed mushrooms and onions. Cool, beat egg yolks and fold into mixture. Sauté mushroom caps in remaining tablespoon of margarine. Place in casserole lightly rubbed with melted margarine, hollow side up. Fold stiffly beaten egg whites into cooled mixture. Pour over mushroom caps. Sprinkle with Parmesan cheese. Bake at 375° about 30 minutes, or until puffed and brown.

BAKED TOMATO WITH SPINACH PURÉE
(For four)

2 medium-size tomatoes, cut in half
$1^{1}/_{2}$ pounds fresh spinach
1 tablespoon chopped onion
$1/2$ cup skim milk
salt substitute and white pepper
Parmesan cheese

Wash spinach, place in saucepan with onion. Heat

Skim off fat and return meat to broth. Slice thin and serve with broth, seasoned to your taste. I like to serve little white onions with this, so I add them to the broth to cook. Or I cook the beef in canned consommé and water, half and half.

CHEESE CUSTARD
(For four)

This is a wonderful luncheon dish.

4 egg yolks
1^1/$_2$ cups skim milk
1^1/$_2$ cups grated Swiss cheese
^{1}/$_8$ teaspoon nutmeg
salt substitute
4 egg whites

Beat egg yolks, add skim milk, cheese, nutmeg and salt substitute to taste. Fold in stiffly beaten egg whites. Pour into shallow casserole. Bake at 350° for 30 minutes.

OVEN-BAKED FRESH SALMON
(For four)

^{1}/$_4$ cup lemon juice
1 teaspoon grated lemon peel
1 clove garlic, crushed
^{1}/$_2$ teaspoon paprika
1 teaspoon chopped chives
4 6-ounce salmon steaks

Mix lemon juice, peel, garlic and paprika. Rub over salmon and place on oven broiling pan. Bake at 350° for 20 minutes. Baste. Then turn on broiler and brown. Sprinkle on chives just before serving. Serve with a twist of lemon and Swedish cucumbers.

SWEDISH CUCUMBERS
(For four)

4 cucumbers, peeled and sliced very thin
white wine vinegar to cover
6 scallions (green onions) sliced thin
$1/2$ teaspoon dill seed, or a few sprigs of fresh
    dill
$1/4$ teaspoon artificial sweetener

Place all the ingredients in a bowl. Cover and refrigerate for several hours.

TINOLA
(For four)

1 3-pound chicken cut in quarters
4 whole raw carrots
4 whole white onions
4 pieces celery
1 cup cooked (fresh or frozen) green beans (or
    leave out if you wish)

Wash chicken well. Drain. Place in deep kettle. Add water to cover. Add carrots, onions and celery. Simmer at medium heat until chicken is done, about 1 hour. Let stand until fat comes to top. Remove and add green vegetables. Reheat. Serve with vegetables and

broth. If you feel like splurging on carbohydrates, add a little rice. Not much, though.

SINGAPORE TURKEY BREAST

    1 4-to-6-pound turkey breast (or you may use
      whole turkey)
    1 tablespoon curry powder
    1 tablespoon fines herbes, dried — Spice Is-
      land
    1 tablespoon salt substitute
    1 teaspoon paprika
    1 cup gin
    1 cup water
    1 onion
    1 carrot
    1 piece celery
    1/2 orange

Wash and dry turkey breast. Mix curry powder, herbs, salt substitute and paprika. Rub turkey inside and out with this mixture. Place in pan with vegetables and orange. Roast uncovered at 350° for 3 hours, or until tender. Baste with the gin and water. When done spoon off all fat from juices. Serve sliced thin with the pan juices unthickened.

MARINATED BEETS
(For four)

    1 can whole baby beets or
    2 cups freshly cooked beets (still better)
    1/2 cup red wine vinegar
    1 piece fresh dill
    1 whole onion
    few drops of artificial sweetener

Combine and refrigerate as long as you wish. Add whole hard-cooked eggs for pickled eggs.

JELLIED CUCUMBER SALAD
(For four)

1 tablespoon unflavored gelatin
1/2 cup cold water
1 tablespoon grated onion
1 1/2 cups coarsely grated cucumber
2 tablespoons vinegar
1 tablespoon prepared horseradish

Dissolve gelatin in cold water. Melt over hot water and add rest of ingredients. Pour into individual molds. Refrigerate, unmold on Boston lettuce.

GERMAN COLE SLAW

1 head red or white cabbage
2 tablespoons finely chopped onion (or leave
   it out)
1/4 cup cider vinegar
3 tablespoons chopped parsley
2 tablespoons vegetable salad oil
Cracked pepper

Shred cabbage as fine as possible. Cover with boiling water for 5 minutes. Drain dry. Add rest of ingredients and toss lightly. Serve warm.

YOGURT REMOULADE

1 cup yogurt
1/4 cup chopped parsley
1/2 teaspoon tarragon
2 tablespoons finely chopped onion
1 teaspoon prepared mustard
1 tablespoon chopped capers

Mix and refrigerate. Good with all seafoods. 25

RELISH SALAD BOWL
(For four)

1 can artichoke hearts, cut in half
1/2 pound sliced raw mushrooms
4 whole tomatoes, peeled and quartered
1 cucumber sliced thin (you may omit)
1/4 cup toasted sesame seeds
1 head Romaine broken into pieces

Toss lightly and sprinkle with wine vinegar dressing.

JELLIED SPRING SALAD
(For four or six)

1 package lime Jello or D-Zerta
1 1/2 cups hot water
2 tablespoons vinegar
1 cup finely shredded cabbage
1 cup finely chopped celery
1/2 cup finely shredded cucumber
1/4 cup chopped pimiento

Dissolve Jello in hot water. Cool. Add vinegar and rest of ingredients. When it begins to congeal, pour into a ring mold. Refrigerate several hours. Unmold on salad greens. Serve with yogurt dressing.

SPINACH AND MUSHROOM SALAD
(For four)

1 quart crisp raw spinach leaves
1 cup sliced raw mushrooms
2 tablespoons pine nuts

Sprinkle with salt substitute and a little tarragon vinegar and toss.

STEWED APPLES AND MANDARIN ORANGES
(For four)

4 Rome Beauty or Winesap apples
1/2 lemon sliced thin
2 cups water
1 teaspoon artificial sweetener

Peel and quarter apples. Add with peelings and lemon to water and sweetener. Simmer until tender. Cool and strain. Serve warm or cold. For variety, add canned Mandarin orange sections. The peelings give a pretty pink tinge to the fruit. Use these apples, sprinkled with prepared horseradish, as an accompaniment to broiled chicken.

POTS DE CRÈME
(For four or six)

3 egg yolks
1 cup skim milk
1/4 teaspoon vanilla extract or dark rum
1 teaspoon instant coffee (or not)
artificial sweetener to taste

Beat egg yolks until lemon-colored. Beat in skim milk with vanilla and instant coffee. Sweeten to your taste. Pour into *pots* or custard cups. Cover and bake in pan 3/4 full of water for 1 hour at 325°.

If you are one who enjoys ice cream desserts, invest in an ice cream freezer and make your own. Turning either by hand or by electricity, you can make better low-calorie ices and ice cream than you can buy. It will give your family something to do, also. The 2-quart size is the most practical. The usual proportion of ice to rock salt for freezing is 8 parts ice to 1 part salt.

27

LEMON ICE

4 cups water
2 teaspoons artificial sweetener (but taste for
    sure, as they are all different)
$^3/_4$ cup lemon juice
1 tablespoon grated lemon rind

Mix together and freeze in crank freezer or in refrigerator tray in your deep freeze. I like to take it out of the deep freeze when partially frozen and whip by hand or in an electric blender. For orange ice, use 3 cups orange juice, $^1/_4$ cup lemon juice, grated rind of 2 oranges, and the sweetener to taste. For lime ice, the same preparations as for lemon.

THREE FRUIT SHERBET

$1^1/_2$ cups orange juice
$^3/_4$ cup lemon juice
$1^1/_2$ cups mashed bananas (3)
3 cups water
2 cups skim milk
artificial sweetener to taste

Mix all the ingredients and freeze the same way as the ice. The sherbet can be frozen then packed in a mold, to be more decorative. Unmold on a silver tray and decorate with orange sections and green leaves.

ENGLISH CUSTARD

2 egg yolks
2 cups skim milk
1 egg white
lemon or vanilla extract
artificial sweetener to your taste

Mix egg yolks and skim milk. Cook over low heat

until thickened. Cool and flavor to your taste. Beat and fold in the beaten egg white.

PEARS OR PEACHES POACHED IN RED WINE
(For four)

4 whole pears or peaches peeled
$3/4$ cup water
$1/4$ cup red wine
1 piece lemon rind
1 small piece of cinnamon stick

Drop pears or peaches in water and wine with lemon rind and cinnamon stick. Simmer until soft. Remove fruit and sweeten the syrup to your taste. Pour over the fruit and serve, well chilled or hot.

SECOND
WEEK

The second week the world will look brighter because you will have lost from three to five pounds, depending on how faithful you were to your regime. The skirt or trousers, as the case may be, has dropped a bit by now, so do not slip back to your old eating habits.

FIRST DAY

Lunch

Cold sliced turkey
Jellied Bing cherries
Celery stalk filled with mashed cottage cheese,

flavored with a little prepared horesradish and chopped parsley

Dinner

Half of small ripe cantaloupe (pour hot chicken consommé in it at the table)

Pan-broiled veal T-bone steak, or the nearest thing to it you can get. (Use a Teflon skillet of course. Baste with sherry if you like. I do!)

Jumbo asparagus, fresh or frozen, cooked merely fork-tender, with chopped mushrooms simmered in bouillon sprinkled over

Boiled fresh leeks with lemon juice and chives

Raspberry sponge pudding

SECOND DAY

Lunch (those bridge girls again)

Cheese soufflé

Boston lettuce, grapefruit sections and chopped chives salad

Espresso Granité

Dinner

Fresh tomato juice served in the living room. Put it in a tall stemmed wine glass, celery stick to stir it with.

Leg of lamb roasted with rosemary

Slices of yellow and green squash mixed together with pimiento sauce (such a pretty vegetable!)

Raw vegetable salad with Zesty Dressing

Lemon Snow Pudding Ring filled with season-ripened fruits

THIRD DAY

Lunch

Hot chicken broth with feathered egg white and
slices of water chestnuts (just stir raw egg white
into hot broth with a fork). A green salad bowl
with slivers of cold meat and Swiss cheese with
minted salad dressing

It is time now to entertain and a wonderful time to
do it. Your friends will enjoy the change in pace also.
Either you have a built-in conversation piece or you
may keep the fact that the meal is lower in calories
a secret, and take the bows as they compliment you
. . . and they will.

Dinner

Cold tomato and shrimp soup
Fresh ginger roasted rib eye of beef
Salsify (oyster plant)
Pea pods, mushrooms and celery
Endive and sliced radish salad
Lemon juice and oil dressing
Old-fashioned prune whip with hot orange custard

Serve a dry red Bordeaux — one glass won't hurt you.

FOURTH DAY

Lunch

Red ripe tomato filled with cottage cheese scramble
Poached cinnamony apple

Dinner

Slices of papaya with fresh lime
Breast of chicken Hunter Style
Whole cauliflower, Parmesan
Slivered green beans with sliced water chestnuts
My favorite cole slaw
Coffee sponge

FIFTH DAY

Lunch

Picnic lunch around the pool! Invite your calorie-conscious friends. If it rains, eat inside and play poker. Here's something much more exciting than Metrecal:

Thin slices of jellied veal
Eggs deviled with red caviar
Tomatoes filled with diced cucumbers and fresh
  dill
Cold boiled shrimp on ice
Slices of fresh pineapple dusted with chopped mint

Dinner

Hot broiled grapefruit, flavored with sherry and
  a bit of honey
Broiled King Crab leg (rub with whipped margarine
  and soy sauce before broiling)
Canned artichoke hearts and mushrooms with
  pimiento sauce
Zucchini fans
Cold lemon soufflé with puréed apricots

SIXTH DAY

Lunch

With the family around the house (because who doesn't stay at home on Saturday?) you might serve:

French Veal Sauté (serve on green noodles for the rest of the family)
Wax bean and bean sprout salad bowl
Watermelon (small piece for you)

Dinner on the Terrace

Consommé on the Rocks, served with a tray of pickled shrimp
Chopped steaks (hamburgers), charcoal-broiled
Baked green tomatoes and onion rings Parmesan
Celery hearts and radishes or any raw vegetables in a flower pot of ice
Buttermilk sherbet

It goes without saying, your family will make an old-fashioned hamburger out of the chopped steak, so no worries about them.

SEVENTH DAY

Lunch

Pot au Feu

Sunday Night Supper

Chicken and snow peas on rice
Green salad with slices of hearts of palm, garlic dressing
Fresh stewed peach

RECIPES YOU WILL NEED

JELLIED BING CHERRIES
(For four)

1 cup water-pack Bing cherry juice
1 teaspoon gelatin
Cherries from the Number 2 can, about 1 cup
1 teaspoon grated orange peel

Dissolve the gelatin in $1/4$ cup of the juice. Bring the rest of juice to a boil and add to the softened gelatin. Cool. When partially congealed, add cherries and orange peel. Pour into individual molds or a pint-size ring. Refrigerate overnight.

RAW VEGETABLE SALAD
(For four)

$1/2$ cup bean sprouts, fresh or canned
1 head Boston lettuce
$1/2$ cup sliced raw mushrooms
$1/2$ cup raw cauliflower buds
$1/4$ cup crisp cooked fresh green beans
$1/2$ cup sliced water chestnuts

Wash the bean sprouts and drain. Separate lettuce leaves and break into a bowl. Add rest of ingredients and toss with

ZESTY DRESSING

$1/2$ cup wine vinegar
4 tablespoons salad oil
1 tablespoon chili sauce
$1/2$ teaspoon paprika
1 teaspoon mixed dried herbs
1 clove garlic crushed
1 teaspoon cracked pepper

WAX BEAN SALAD
(For four)

1 Number 2 can French-cut wax beans drained
1 can bean sprouts, drained
$1/2$ cup diced celery
$1/2$ cup sliced radishes
2 tablespoons diced pimiento

Mix and place in a shallow pan. Cover with

$1/2$ cup white wine vinegar
1 tablespoon soy sauce
$1/4$ cup salad oil
a little artificial sweetener

Chill several hours. Spoon into a bowl of crisp salad greens.

GARLIC DRESSING
(2 cups)

2 teaspoons dry mustard
1 teaspoon salt substitute
$1/4$ cup flour
1 clove garlic crushed
$1^1/_3$ cups skim milk or water
2 eggs
$3/4$ cup white wine vinegar
2 tablespoons whipped margarine
artificial sweetener to taste

Mix dry ingredients with garlic. Add skim milk. Stir until smooth. Cook over hot water until thickened. Add eggs and beat. Cook 3 minutes. Remove and add rest of ingredients.

MINT DRESSING FOR SALADS OR VEGETABLES

 $^1/_2$ cup vegetable salad oil
 $^1/_4$ cup red wine vinegar
 $^1/_2$ cup fresh mint leaves finely chopped
 1 garlic bud, crushed
 $^1/_2$ teaspoon cracked pepper
 1 teaspoon salt substitute

Put in a container and shake. Very good on cold
artichokes, fresh or canned. Add grated lemon peel
for Lemon Mint variation.

COLD TOMATO AND SHRIMP SOUP
(For six)

 1 10-ounce can beef bouillon
 $^1/_4$ cup diced cucumber
 $^1/_2$ cup diced peeled and "seeded" fresh tomato
 2 tablespoons wine vinegar
 1 cup diced cooked shrimp
 1 teaspoon finely chopped onion

Mix, chill and serve. It is a pretty soup and could be
served in scooped-out tomatoes.

BOILED FRESH LEEKS
(For four)

Cut off the roots of 4 leeks and leave only 2 inches
of the leaves. Cut in half lengthwise. Wash thoroughly
under cold running water. Place in a skillet, cover with
boiling water. Cover and cook over low heat for 15 or
20 minutes or until tender. Sprinkle with chopped
chives and lemon juice.

CAULIFLOWER

Cauliflower should be washed carefully under running
water. Fortunately, our produce men do some of the

cleaning for us. It always looks better when served whole, so put in a deep kettle and cover with boiling water and a little skim milk. Cover and cook about 20 minutes. Don't overcook. Drain and sprinkle with Parmesan cheese or toasted sesame seeds.

PIMIENTO SAUCE FOR VEGETABLES

1 canned pimiento chopped fine
1 clove garlic crushed (you may omit)
1/2 cup finely diced celery
1 teaspoon finely diced onion

Mix, season with white pepper and salt substitute and spoon over any green vegetable.

SALSIFY

Salsify or oyster plant is available in Number 2 cans. It is fairly expensive, but worth the price. It satisfies those who wish potatoes, and people who are not familiar with it will think it is potato. Merely take from the can, drain and heat. I like to heat it in skim milk, drain and add chopped parsley for color. It is nice combined with green beans, too.

PEA PODS, MUSHROOMS AND CELERY
(For four)

1 cup thin-sliced celery cut on the bias (I call it "slanty-eyed")
1/2 cup thin-sliced canned mushrooms
1 cup pea pods, fresh or canned
2 tablespoons skim milk

Boil celery covered for 1 minute. Don't guess — 1 minute. Drain. Cook pea pods the same length of time if fresh. If canned, drain well. Combine all three with the skim milk. Simmer 2 minutes. Sprinkle with parsley.

ZUCCHINI

Zucchini squash is a great diet vegetable. If cooked correctly, it has a bright fresh color. You can slice thin, add a little chopped onion, place in a skillet with very little water. Cover and cook for 5 minutes. Do yellow squash the same way. Mix for a pretty dish.

Zucchini fans are pretty too. Select small squash, cut lengthwise, keeping the squash together at the blossom end. Cook the same way. Remove and spread slices in a fan shape. Use any sauce or just cracked pepper.

BAKED GREEN TOMATO AND ONION RING
(For four)

  2 large green tomatoes
  1 large white onion partially cooked
  1 tablespoon whipped margarine
  2 tablespoons Parmesan cheese

Cut tomatoes in half. Cover with onion cut in 4 thick slices. Place in a shallow casserole and add the margarine and cheese. Bake at 350° until the tomato is soft and the onion brown.

CHEESE SOUFFLÉ
(For four or six)

  4 tablespoons whipped margarine
  6 tablespoons all purpose flour
  1¹/₂ cups hot skim milk
  ¹/₄ teaspoon white pepper
  1 teaspoon prepared mustard — this gives it pazazz
  3 drops Tabasco
  1 cup grated Cheddar or Swiss cheese
  8 eggs

Melt margarine, add flour, cook until bubbly. Add   41 hot skim milk and seasonings. Bring to a boil, stirring constantly. Boil 1 minute — count it! — still stirring. Remove and slightly cool. Add cheese and egg yolks beaten until thick. Cool and fold in stiffly beaten egg whites. Pour into lightly greased soufflé dish. Bake at 300° until a knife inserted in the center comes out clean.

LEG OF LAMB WITH ROSEMARY
(For six or eight)

1 4-to-5-pound leg of lamb, bone in
1 teaspoon salt substitute
1 teaspoon paprika
2 tablespoons dried or fresh rosemary
$^1/_4$ cup chopped onion
2 cups dry white wine

Rub lamb with salt, paprika and rosemary. Place on top of the onions in a roasting pan. Roast uncovered at 300°. Baste with the wine several times until wine is gone. Roast 2 hours for rare, 3 hours for medium, longer for well-done. If you do not know the flavor of pink lamb, cultivate it. You'll enjoy it. Slice thin and serve with strained pan juices.

BREAST OF CHICKEN HUNTER STYLE
(For four)

4 4-to-5-ounce chicken breasts
$^1/_4$ cup sliced mushrooms
1 tablespoon thinly sliced green onion
$^1/_2$ cup dry white wine
1 cup canned chicken consommé
1 tablespoon chopped parsley
$^1/_2$ cup peeled chopped tomato, no seeds

Skin the breasts and sauté in a Teflon skillet until light
42 brown. Remove, add mushrooms and onion. Sauté

1 minute. Add wine, cook 1 minute more, and add consommé with parsley and tomato. Add chicken and simmer until slightly thickened. Cover and place in 350° oven for 10 minutes. This is a quick dinner and everyone will enjoy it. It takes about 20 minutes to do it.

FRENCH VEAL SAUTÉ
(For four)

1¹/₂ pounds lean veal stew meat
1 tablespoon salad oil
¹/₂ cup sliced canned mushrooms
¹/₄ clove garlic
¹/₂ cup chopped onion
¹/₄ cup slivered green pepper
1 cup canned tomatoes, mashed or fresh, peeled and chopped
¹/₂ cup Burgundy wine

Sauté meat in oil until a light brown on all sides. Remove meat, add mushrooms, garlic and onion. Sauté until onion is limp. Add green peppers, tomatoes, wine and meat. Cover and cook at low heat for about 1¹/₂ hours. Add water if necessary, but cook until meat is tender. Sprinkle with chopped parsley and season with salt substitute and cracked pepper.

POT AU FEU
(For four)

1¹/₂ pounds lean beef round or top butt
4 leeks, sliced
4 small onions, each stuck with a clove
1 cup sliced carrots
1 bay leaf
2 peppercorns

Cover beef with water in deep kettle. Cook just under   43 boiling for 2 hours. Add rest of ingredients and cook until carrots are tender. Serve thin slices of beef with the broth and vegetables.

JELLIED VEAL
(For four or six)

1 pound veal stew meat, cut in fine dice
1³/₄ cups chicken broth
¹/₂ cup white wine
1 bay leaf
1 tablespoon gelatin
1 cup finely chopped parsley
1 scallion chopped fine

Cover veal with water and cook until tender, about 1 hour. Heat chicken broth and wine with bay leaf for 30 minutes. Season with salt substitute and white pepper. Add the gelatin softened in a little of the broth before heating. Divide in half and add veal to half of this mixture as it begins to thicken, then spread in a shallow casserole. Add parsley and shallots to rest of gelatin mixture and pour over veal. Cool overnight in refrigerator.

CHICKEN AND PEA PODS
(For four)

4 4-to-5-ounce chicken breasts
1 tablespoon vegetable oil
¹/₄ cup sliced celery
¹/₄ cup sliced bamboo shoots, or leave out
¹/₄ cup sliced water chestnuts
1 cup pea pods
2 teaspoons soy sauce
¹/₂ teaspoon Accent
1 cup chicken broth
1 tablespoon cornstarch or arrowroot
2 tablespoons cold water

Remove skin from chicken, and cut meat into strips. Sauté in the oil. Add rest of ingredients except cornstarch and water. Cover and cook 5 minutes. Blend cornstarch and water and add to mixture. Cook and stir until thickened. Serve at once.

One nice thing about this, you can do all the preparation in advance then combine.

————————•————————

Desserts for dieters should be as pretty as a picture. These taste good as well.

RASPBERRY SPONGE PUDDING
(For four)

1 cup skim milk
4 egg yolks
$1/2$ teaspoon vanilla
2 cups fresh or frozen raspberries
4 egg whites

Combine milk, yolks of eggs in top of a double boiler. Cook until custard is thick. Remove. Add vanilla and cool. Rub berries through a sieve or put in blender. Add to custard. Sweeten to your taste with artificial sweetener. Beat egg whites stiff and fold into custard. Serve in cold stemmed crystal, or pass and let everyone help themselves.

You can do many things with Snow Pudding to keep your spirits up and your family guessing, and it always looks so refreshing. I prefer to make it in a ring and fill it with fresh fruit in season, and pass a custard sauce made with skim milk and vary its flavoring. For guests, I pour 2 tablespoons ignited brandy on the fruit before letting them sample it, but be sure they see you.

It's no fun to do it in the kitchen. This is definitely a serve-in-the-dining-room dessert.

LEMON SNOW PUDDING RING
(For eight)

2 tablespoons gelatin
$1/4$ cup cold water
$2^1/2$ cups boiling water
$1/2$ cup lemon juice
2 teaspoons grated lemon peel
artificial sweetener
6 egg whites

Dissolve gelatin in cold water. Add boiling water and stir until gelatin is completely melted. Cool. Add lemon juice and grated lemon peel. Add sweetener to taste. When the mixture begins to thicken, fold in the stiffly beaten egg whites. Pour into a 2-quart ring mold. Refrigerate until firm. Unmold and fill center with fruit. You may add food coloring to the mixture if you are so inclined.

ESPRESSO GRANITÉ

$1^1/2$ cups Espresso coffee
2 quarts water
2 cups cold water
artificial sweetener

Pour 2 quarts boiling water over Espresso. Let stand for 5 minutes. Strain if you do not make it in a drip coffeepot. Add cold water and sweeten. Put in refrigerator tray in deep freeze to freeze. Take out twice and whip. Serve in tall wine glasses.

OLD-FASHIONED PRUNE WHIP
(For six)

1 cup puréed cooked prunes or use prune baby
   food
2 tablespoons lemon juice
5 egg whites
artificial sweetener

Mix prunes and lemon juice. Sweeten to your taste.
Beat egg whites until stiff and fold into the prune mix-
ture. Pile into a large crystal bowl and serve with
Orange Custard.

COFFEE SPONGE
(For four)

1 tablespoon plus 1 teaspoon gelatin
1 cup skim milk
1½ cups coffee
3 egg yolks
artificial sweetener
3 egg whites

Dissolve gelatin in ¼ cup cold coffee. Heat milk.
Add to gelatin. Add coffee and sweeten to your taste.
Add beaten egg yolks. Cool. As it begins to congeal,
fold in stiffly beaten egg whites. Pile into a straight-
sided soufflé dish and serve into crystal bowls. Use
instant coffee!

One of the most popular desserts at The Greenhouse is

BUTTERMILK SHERBET

4 cups buttermilk
¾ cup lemon juice
1 cup corn syrup
6 tablespoons grated lemon peel
artificial sweetener to your taste

Mix all ingredients and freeze. When fresh strawberries are ripe, add 1 cup of puréed strawberries and cut the lemon juice to $1/4$ cup. The same with peaches, but they must be ripe. You can dress it up for company too. Pile the plain sherbet in half of a fresh or stewed peach, and pour puréed strawberries over. Slip a green leaf from the yard under the dessert crystal.

STEWED FRUIT

Fresh raw fruit does not always agree with everyone's body chemistry, but it is an excellent way to cut down on calories. Freshly cooked fruit agrees with everyone. The simplest method is to drop fruit, like apples, apricots, peaches, pears and plums, into boiling sweetened water, add a few slices of lemon or orange, and simmer until soft. They should always retain their form, so again, for good flavor and texture, don't overcook. You may peel or not, depending on how you like it. I think a beautiful stewed peach is a lovely dessert to end any meal, or it is nice to serve a compote of mixed stewed fruits. I always serve a slice of the lemon or orange that has cooked with them. You may add whatever spices you like while cooking — no added calories!

COLD LEMON SOUFFLÉ
(For four or six)

1 tablespoon gelatin
$1/4$ cup cold water
2 cups skim milk
4 egg yolks
artificial sweetener
$1/2$ cup lemon juice
2 tablespoons grated lemon peel
8 egg whites

Dissolve gelatin in cold water. Bring milk to a boil, add

egg yolks and beat. Cook until thick. Add gelatin. Cool. Add sweetener and lemon juice and peel. As mixture begins to congeal, fold in stiffly beaten egg whites. Pile in soufflé dish and refrigerate. Do the same for orange or lime soufflé, using these juices and peel in place of the lemon.

4

THIRD
WEEK

The third week makes you wonder why you ever did eat too much. You feel better, you can pick up things from the floor without losing your breath, and thoughts of new clothes make you happier. Too, you aren't as bored as if you had gone the tomato and cottage cheese route. Now it will be harder to lose, but don't give up.

FIRST DAY

Lunch

A low-calorie version of Buca Lapi
Canned artichoke hearts and raw spinach salad
with mint dressing

Dinner

Marinated mushrooms
Orange baked chicken with fresh carrot sticks
Broccoli with grated raw beets sprinkled over
Chilled tomato filled with ratatouille
Hot apricot whip

SECOND DAY

Lunch

Salagamundi eggs
Braised celery
Half grapefruit

Dinner

Fresh vegetable cocktail
Meat loaf baked in an angel food tin. Fill the
    center with baked fresh onion rings
Braised lettuce
Fennel salad
Stewed fresh pear filled with whipped cottage
    cheese

THIRD DAY

Lunch

Cold boiled leeks with Danish shrimp
Zesty French Dressing
Red Delicious apple and sliver of Swiss cheese

Dinner

Tomato Surprise
Roasted rack of lamb with natural gravy
White turnips, parslied
Asparagus with grated lemon peel
Cup custard with puréed strawberries   51

FOURTH DAY

Lunch

Fresh salmon soufflé
Curried pineapple fingers
Raw spinach salad with toasted pine nuts dressed
    with tarragon vinegar and salt substitute

Dinner

Surprise the family, or perhaps drop-ins for a high-ball, with Beef Tartare Balls and hot beef bouillon served in a demitasse cup.

Recently gourmet shops have been featuring a clay "chicken cooker." It is made of clay, undecorated, rather crudely designed, and those made in Italy are the better ones — so far. They are good for diet cooking and are rather fun to bring to the table. You can get large ones for hen and turkeys — and I cook veal and beef in mine — or small ones that will hold a Rock Cornish hen. One good thing about them is that you can leave them in the oven and go play, as the cooking is slow and self-basting. For a small dinner party, the small ones can be used as decoration and also to hold the food.

You merely put whatever you are going to cook in them, with seasonings and a little wine, and put them in the oven at 350°, and when they are finished you bring to the table in the cooker.

Rock Cornish Hens in Clay Cooker
Whipped Jerusalem artichokes
Okra with grated lemon peel
Zucchini salad
Vanilla ice cream in half of fresh peach with
    puréed fruit spilled over

FIFTH DAY

Lunch

Pickled egg salad with canned asparagus spears
Fresh apricots and cherries in ice water

In Italy I had this kind of fruit served in a crystal bowl of ice water. What an idea! Cool and clean at the same time.

Dinner

Jellied borsch with leeks
Mustard broiled Dover Sole
Fennel Sauté
Spinach with orange sections
Sliced hearts of palm and cucumber balls with capers and No-Calorie Dressing
Compote of fruit

SIXTH DAY

Lunch

A big combination salad bowl in preparation for dinner with guests.

Saturday night is a nice night to entertain. Everyone is relaxed after a week of trials. Go the low-calorie route again and serve fresh pineapple frappé on the terrace or wherever you gather. Keep quiet and they may think it is a frozen Bacardi cocktail. I served it at The Greenhouse one night to some husbands of guests. They thought so!

There is an excellent Iceland trout that comes in cans — four or five to the can. I keep a can in my refrigerator at all times for a quick first course.

Dinner

Chilled Iceland trout with mustard sauce, another
  Greenhouse favorite
Peppered beef steak, sirloin or top butt
Sliced carrots in yogurt
Boiled Brussels sprouts with chopped fresh mint
Kentucky Limestone lettuce with sliced canned
  mushrooms
Lemon juice and oil dressing
Spoom

SEVENTH DAY

Lunch

Large fresh crabmeat salad with slices of papaya

Supper Snacks

Garden fresh tomatoes, celery hearts, cottage
  cheese whipped up with grated carrots and
  chives
Boiled beef frankfurter with sauerkraut
Fruit gelatin

RECIPES YOU WILL NEED

MARINATED MUSHROOMS
(For four or six)

1 pound fresh mushrooms
1 pint water
juice of 1 lemon
$^3/_4$ cup tarragon vinegar
1 tablespoon salad oil
1 clove garlic, crushed
1 bay leaf
$^1/_4$ teaspoon thyme
cracked pepper

If mushrooms are large, slice in half with the stem left on. Wash and boil 3 minutes with the water and lemon juice. You start counting when the water begins to boil. Drain. Add rest of ingredients, bring to a boil and pour over mushrooms. Refrigerate. Serve very cold with chopped parsley sprinkled over. You will notice I use chopped parsley a great deal, for color and for flavor — no calories. Chop a whole bunch, put in a glass jar and seal. Use when you need it. It will keep several days.

FRESH VEGETABLE COCKTAIL
(For four)

$1/2$ cup finely diced raw carrot
$1/2$ cup finely diced celery
1 tablespoon diced green pepper
$1/2$ cup diced fresh tomato
$1/2$ cup diced raw cauliflower (or any other un-
    cooked vegetable)

Serve well chilled in stemmed glasses with cocktail sauce spooned over.

COCKTAIL SAUCE

$1/2$ cup catsup
1 tablespoon prepared horseradish or grated
    fresh
1 tablespoon vinegar
$1/2$ cup chili sauce
2 tablespoons lemon juice
2 tablespoons finely minced celery

Mix and refrigerate. Use for any seafood also.

RATATOUILLE
(For four or six)

1 medium eggplant peeled, sliced thin
1 seeded green pepper sliced thin
1 seeded peeled ripe tomato
1 onion sliced thin
1 tablespoon olive oil
1 teaspoon lemon juice
salt substitute
white pepper

Pile vegetables in layers in a casserole. Add oil and lemon juice. Sprinkle with salt substitute and white pepper. Bake at 300° until vegetables are cooked through. Refrigerate and pile in scooped-out peeled tomatoes or serve hot as a vegetable. The menfolk like it, especially those who say they dislike eggplant.

TOMATO SURPRISE
(For four)

4 ripe tomatoes, chopped fine
4 tablespoons grated onion
salt substitute and pepper

Freeze until mushy in deep freeze. Stir frequently. Serve in cocktail glasses or the scooped-out tomato. Flavor yogurt with curry and spoon on top.

BEEF TARTARE BALLS
(For six)

1 pound tender beef trimmed of all fat and finely ground
1 egg yolk
1 teaspoon fresh onion juice
$1/2$ teaspoon white pepper
1 teaspoon salt substitute

Mix, form into balls and roll in chopped parsley and decorate with capers if you like.

JELLIED BORSCH WITH LEEKS
(For four)

2 teaspoons gelatin
$1/2$ cup finely chopped beets (canned)
1 tablespoon grated onion
$1/4$ cup finely minced celery
1 cup beef juice (add water if necessary)
1 cup beef consommé
2 teaspoons lemon juice
$1/4$ cup thinly sliced leeks

Dissolve gelatin in $1/4$ cup of the beet juice. Simmer beets, juice, onions, celery and consommé for 20 minutes. Remove and cool. Add lemon juice and season if necessary. Simmer leeks in very little water until soft. Add to mixture. Allow to jell in refrigerator.

FENNEL SALAD
(For four)

My favorite of all low-calorie salads. You cannot find it in the markets all year round, so when you see it, use it. It looks like an overgrown bunch of celery and smells like anise. Keep it around as an in-between snack! No calories!

2 medium-sized fennel
2 tablespoons salad oil
4 tablespoons wine vinegar
2 hard-cooked egg whites
2 tablespoons capers
2 tablespoons chopped parsley

Place fennel in ice water for 1 hour. Remove, dry and slice very thin. Cover with ice to ensure crispness.

Mix oil, vinegar, egg whites chopped fine, capers and parsley. When ready to serve, remove fennel from ice. Drain and toss with the dressing.

The bulb end of the fennel is used for cooking. Boil with a slice of lemon until fork tender. Remove and slice. Place in a skillet. Sprinkle with salt substitute, Parmesan cheese and chopped chives. Cover and simmer until cheese is melted through. Nice with beef too.

LEEKS

Almost any gourmet cookbook will mention leeks and shrimp together. You may buy the tiny Danish shrimp in cans, or, at times, frozen. If you live on the West Coast, the bay shrimp are as acceptable. Anyhow, cook the leeks which have been split in half lengthwise, drain and chill. Pile the shrimp on top, just about as many as you like. Serve with Zesty Dressing.

SPINACH

Raw spinach is a nice change in pace for salads and the markets have fresh supplies for the most part of the year. Wash it carefully, remove the stems and refrigerate to crisp. Add any low-calorie vegetable, and I like to toss a few, very few, toasted pine nuts in with it. Then I merely sprinkle with salt substitute and tarragon vinegar. Try it!

Vary the way you serve spinach, by merely melting it (cook 3 to 5 minutes) and toss with Mandarin or Sunkist orange sections.

COMBINATION SALAD BOWL
(For two)

1 cup sliced raw zucchini
1 cup sliced raw mushrooms
1 cup cooked snipped green beans
1 tomato, peeled and quartered
1 bunch watercress
1 head Boston lettuce cut in quarters
2 hard-cooked eggs, sliced

Toss with wine vinegar dressing.

CRABMEAT SALAD
(For two)

1½ cups crabmeat
½ cup finely diced celery
Yogurt dressing to moisten
chopped parsley

Fresh crabmeat is in the markets most of the year and is low in calories. Mix with celery and yogurt dressing and pile on lettuce leaves. Garnish with chopped parsley. Serve with slices of papaya or melon.

PINEAPPLE FRAPPÉ
(For six)

2 cups fresh pineapple, ripe
1 cup ice
a few mint leaves

Put in blender at high speed. Serve at once in well-chilled stemmed glasses. Repeat for a second round. Be sure when you buy pineapple that it is ripe. It will not ripen anywhere except on the bush.

MUSTARD SAUCE

2 egg yolks
$^1/_2$ teaspoon dry mustard
6 tablespoons cider vinegar
2 tablespoons skim milk
1 tablespoon prepared mustard
1 tablespoon lemon juice
artificial sweetener

Beat egg yolks with mustard over hot water. Add vinegar and beat. Cook until thick. Add milk and continue beating. You should have a French Whip. Cook 5 minutes. Cool, add mustard and lemon juice and artificial sweetener if desired. This is good for dressing hot vegetables also.

BAKED ONION RINGS
(For four)

3 large white onions
1 cup water
chopped parsley

Slice onions as thin as possible. Place in shallow casserole and cover with water. Bake in a 300° oven until soft and all the water has evaporated. Add chopped parsley and season to your taste.

BRAISED LETTUCE

Wash and trim a head of Iceberg lettuce. Cover with beef consommé. Cover and cook until tender, but not soft. Cut in fourths to serve. Do celery the same way. Anyone who is interested in having vegetables taste good without too much worry in cooking them should invest in a steamette. Houseware counters and gourmet shops usually carry them or should. You merely put the vegetable to be cooked in the steamette and place in a pot of boiling water, being careful not to have the water come over the vegetable. Cover with the cover designed for the pot, or with foil, and cook. It takes about 4 minutes for fresh green beans. You really capture the flavor of fresh vegetables with this gadget. I use it for thin slices of turnips, asparagus, broccoli, any fresh vegetable except tomatoes.

ASPARAGUS

I am one of the best fans that fresh asparagus has. I cool off a bit with the frozen kind, and the canned leaves me cold regardless of whether it is white or green. Perhaps because of being brought up with asparagus growing in profusion in my family's back yard, I dream about it when it is out of season. Anyhow, it is an excellent low-calorie vegetable and really does not need Hollandaise or butter to enhance its flavor.

If fresh, remove "scales" with a paring knife or vegetable peeler. Wash many times in cold water to remove the sand that sticks like mad to the scales and ridges. Break the white part off, lay in a shallow pan, cover with water and boil until tender, or tie in bunches and stand in a deep pot. Either way do not overcook; from 8 to 12 minutes is enough. Or slice on the bias in thin slices and cook only 4 minutes. If frozen, place still frozen in a skillet. Cover and cook until the ice melts and then 2 minutes more. Dress with grated orange, lemon or lime, riced egg white, or sprinkle with Parmesan cheese, a version of Buca Lapi. Parmesan cheese is low in calories and can be used in place of butter on any green vegetable. In fact, I prefer it since I am calorie-conscious.

WHIPPED JERUSALEM ARTICHOKES
(For four)

1 pound Jerusalem artichokes
$1/2$ cup skim milk

Peel and cook artichokes in boiling water for 30 minutes, or until tender. Remove. Put in blender with milk and whip, or mash by hand. Sprinkle with parsley or dill.

ZUCCHINI SALAD
(For four)

1 clove garlic
1 head Boston lettuce
1 head Romaine
2 uncooked zucchini
12 peeled cherry tomatoes
garlic dressing

Rub bowl with garlic dressing. Break lettuce and Romaine into bowl. Add zucchini thinly sliced and tomatoes. Dribble dressing through and toss. The Herb Green Dressing is good on this also.

SLICED CARROTS IN YOGURT
(For six)

6 medium-size carrots
1 cup yogurt
grated orange peel

Scrape and cook carrots in boiling water till tender, or use steamette. Remove and slice. Season. Reheat until hot, pour 1 cup yogurt over and sprinkle with grated orange peel.

ORANGE BAKED CHICKEN
(For four)

2 1½-pound roasting chickens
3 tablespoons minced shallots
½ teaspoon paprika
¼ teaspoon dried rosemary
¼ teaspoon salt substitute
¼ teaspoon white pepper
1 cup fresh orange juice

Wash and dry chickens. Place in a shallow oven-proof casserole and rub with the seasonings mixed with the shallots. Place in a 300° oven and baste frequently with the orange juice until chicken is brown, about 1 hour. Peel, cook and cut fresh carrots into fingers and brown in the pan juices. An interesting flavor.

SALAGAMUNDI EGGS
(For one serving)

2 tablespoons slivered onion
2 tablespoons chopped tomato
2 cans sliced mushrooms
2 eggs
salt substitute
cracked pepper

Simmer onion and tomato for 2 minutes in Teflon skillet. Add mushrooms and heat. Beat 2 eggs into skillet and stir rapidly until cooked as hard as you like your eggs. Season and sprinkle cracked pepper over; sometimes I sprinkle Parmesan cheese over it. Also, sometimes add a little left-over meat.

Meat loaf baked in an angel food tin makes a dinner fit for a king. No one will believe it is meat loaf — is meat loaf not always in a loaf?

MEAT LOAF
(For six)

- 2 pounds ground beef
- 2 tablespoons melted whipped margarine
- 2 eggs slightly beaten
- 1 cup skim milk
- 2 tablespoons prepared mustard
- 2 tablespoons finely minced onion
- $1/2$ teaspoon white pepper
- 2 teaspoons salt substitute

Mix together and pack in a lightly greased angel food tin (use whipped margarine) or a Teflon tin. Bake at 350° for 45 to 60 minutes, or until it is well browned and shrinks from side of tin. Turn out on a pretty serving tray and fill center with baked onions or mushrooms or both. Decorate with watercress or parsley.

ROAST RACK OF LAMB

I would choose rack of lamb over chops only if I liked roasting better than broiling — and I do. Your butcher will give you the number of chops you desire in one piece. Have him trim off the fat and "French-trim" the ribs. It is also an elegant looking entrée. I like to bring it to the table dolled up with watercress and serve baked fresh peaches with it, when I can get them, otherwise water-packed peach halves, sprinkled with curry and white wine. The juices from cooking are the only sauce necessary.

(For four)

A whole rack has 16 chops. I am allowing 2 chops per person, 1 chop for the dieter.

- 2 tablespoons finely chopped onion
- 2 tablespoons finely chopped celery
- $1/2$ teaspoon rosemary
- $1/2$ cup white wine
- $1/2$ cup bouillon
- $1/2$ cup chopped parsley
- 2 shallots finely minced

Rub rack with salt substitute and white pepper. Roast at 400° for 20 minutes. Drain off any fat. Add onion, celery and rosemary. Lower heat to 350° and roast 20 minutes more. Remove lamb, add wine and bouillon to pan. Let boil for 10 minutes. Mix the parsley and shallots and spread over the meat. Return to oven for 15 minutes more. Cut between the ribs to serve and use the strained pan juices for sauce, but check for seasonings first. Leave in oven a longer period of time for well-done.

SALMON SOUFFLÉ WITH CURRIED PINEAPPLE FINGERS
(For four)

- 3 tablespoons whipped margarine
- 3 tablespoons flour
- 1 cup skim milk
- 1 teaspoon lemon juice
- 2 egg yolks
- 1 cup flaked salmon, fresh or canned
- 3 egg whites

Melt margarine, add flour. Cook until bubbly. Add milk   65 and cook until thick. Add lemon juice and egg yolks and cook for 2 minutes, stirring constantly. Add salmon and cool. Fold in the egg whites stiffly beaten. Turn out in a mold lightly rubbed with margarine.

Fresh or water-packed pineapple rubbed with curry powder and baked, goes well with any fish, especially when you do not serve a sauce with it.

PEPPERED STEAK

Press freshly ground or cracked pepper into a sirloin or top butt steak. Allow a six-to-eight-ounce portion for the dieter. Broil to desired doneness. Sprinkle with salt substitute and chives if you like, or ignite with heated cognac.

BEEF FRANKFURTERS AND SAUERKRAUT
(For two)

4 beef frankfurters
1 Number 2 can sauerkraut
2 tablespoons chopped onion
$1/8$ teaspoon caraway seeds if you like

Drain sauerkraut. Add onion and sauté in Teflon skillet for 5 minutes. Add frankfurters and cover. Simmer at low heat for 30 minutes.

VANILLA ICE CREAM

4 egg yolks
1 quart scalded skim milk
1 teaspoon vanilla
artificial sweetener to your taste

Beat egg yolks until thick. Pour into hot milk beating constantly. Boil until slightly thickened. Strain and cool. Add sweetener and vanilla.

Using it as a basic recipe, you could add 2 tablespoons instant coffee or 1 cup puréed fruit when partially frozen. It goes without saying, any extract could be used for flavoring.

Change your way of serving ice cream. Pack it in orange shells. Buy the most attractive dessert dishes you can find. Use leaves and flowers from your garden to decorate.

HOT APRICOT WHIP
(For four)

1 cup dried apricots
2 slices lemon
4 egg whites
artificial sweetener

Cover apricots with water. Add lemon and simmer until soft. Put through a sieve or in an electric blender. Sweeten to your taste. Fold into beaten egg whites. Pile into dish lightly buttered (with margarine) and bake at 350° for 30 minutes while your are eating your entrée. Lots of wind, my grandmother would have called it, but it satisfies the idea of dessert.

CUP CUSTARD
(For four)

4 egg yolks
2 cups skim milk
artificial sweetener
$1/2$ teaspoon vanilla or lemon flavor

Beat egg yolks till creamy. Add and beat in the milk. Sweeten and pour into molds. Bake in a pan of hot water at 350° until custard is set. Serve cold or warm. You may sprinkle a bit of nutmeg on each cup before baking if you are of that era — I am. I like to pass puréed fruit to spoon over, because it looks more exciting.

SPOOM
(For four)

6 egg whites
2 cups lemon ice (you make this)

Beat egg whites until stiff. Mix the lemon ice into them. Pile in champagne glasses, dribble — and I mean dribble — pink champagne over.

FRUIT GELATIN
(For four)

2 tablespoons cold water
2 teaspoons gelatin
$1/2$ cup boiling water
1 cup fresh orange juice
1 tablespoon lemon juice
$1/2$ cup fresh orange sections
$1/2$ cup fresh berries
$1/2$ cup fresh peaches
       or
$1^1/2$ cups water-packed fruit
artificial sweetener

Dissolve gelatin in cold water. Add boiling water. Cool, add orange and lemon juice. As it begins to congeal, fold in fruit. Allow to congeal in refrigerator.

5

FOURTH
WEEK

You can make it now. You can even go out for dinner or lunch. There is no restaurant in the country that will not honor the fact of your slimming. Order the same as you would at home: a clear soup, a small piece of lean meat, a vegetable without butter or sauce, a salad of greens, and fruit for dessert, but then don't order an ice cream pie like some do at the Zodiac Room in Neiman-Marcus. We offer a slim-line lunch and then, oh my, ice cream pie indeed!

One highball or one glass of wine won't hurt you. You can think of new worlds to conquer, and new clothes, but do not go back to the high-calorie way of life.

FIRST DAY

Lunch

Poached egg in canned or fresh artichoke bottom
Parmesan grilled tomato
Baked pear with lemon sauce

Dinner

Celery hearts vinaigrette
Roast chicken filled with fresh grapes
Boiled leeks mixed with sliced zucchini
Broccoli soufflé with Mock Hollandaise
Wine jelly parfait

SECOND DAY

Lunch

Cold sliced chicken
Pineapple cheese salad
Spanish melon with lime

Dinner

Buttermilk tomato soup
Roast loin or rack of veal
Julienne carrots with chives
Braised endive with shallots and mushrooms
Watercress salad with cucumbers, mustard dress-
    ing
Grapefruit ice in grapefruit shell

THIRD DAY

Lunch

Bouillabaisse salad
Fresh strawberries in brandy snifter

Dinner

I would certainly make this menu do for an occasion. Before dinner, a tray of slices of green pepper, raw Brussels sprouts, radishes and carrot sticks with an interesting low-calorie dip. Sit down to:

Broiled squab
Yellow squash au citron
Cabbage with pine nuts
Molded fruit salad on leaves of Romaine
Eggnog ice cream

FOURTH DAY

Lunch

Meat balls cooked and served in consommé take on a more expensive look. This is always a popular day at The Greenhouse.

2 meat balls cooked in consommé
German cole slaw made with red cabbage and
    served hot, piled high and light
Fresh mango with lime

In serving a mango, peel and stick a fork in the blunt end. This makes it easier to hold as you slice. Serve it whole!

Dinner

Once in a while you should have liver, so have a mixed grill.

Essence of celery soup
Sautéed real calf's liver, small lamb chop, kidney
    and mushrooms
Tomato and eggplant pie
Cold asparagus with garlic dressing
Orange sherbet

FIFTH DAY

Lunch

Fresh artichoke filled with shrimp and hearts of
    palm
Warm baked apple

Dinner

Jellied watercress soup
Poached red snapper with egg sauce
Baby beets with capers
Fresh green beans and salsify
Spinach salad with tomato dressing (diced to-
    matoes added to No-Calorie Dressing)
Steamed fresh peach

SIXTH DAY

Lunch

Tomato aspic ring filled with deviled eggs and
    red caviar
Celery hearts and lots of raw vegetables

And that is enough! To make the aspic use the recipe
for tomato bouillon and add gelatin — 1 tablespoon for
1 pint of liquid.

Dinner

You should have guests now and then!

Cold carrot and orange soup
Broiled tenderloin steak
Spiced onions
Artichoke soufflé ring filled with snipped green
    beans
Salad greens with red hot jelly and raw stuffed
    mushrooms

Floating Island

SEVENTH DAY

Family Dinner at Noon

Slices of honeydew melon with Prosciutto (buy
sliced in cans and use 1 slice only)
Barbecued chicken, could be done out-of-doors
Broccoli Polonnaise
Mexican slaw salad
Lemon ice cream

Late Supper

Cup of garden soup
Fresh grapefruit and strawberries

THE RECIPES

BUTTERMILK TOMATO SOUP

It sounds ghastly, but is good. Don't tell the rest of the
family until they eat it all up.

4 ripe tomatoes quartered
$1/2$ cup water
2 cups buttermilk
salt substitute
watercress
julienne strips of raw carrot
chopped chives

Cook tomatoes in water for 15 minutes. Put through
a sieve or in the blender. Add buttermilk, season and
chill. Decorate with either leaves of watercress, carrot
strips or chopped chives, or all three.

Jellied soups seem like more, so why not use them?
They can look prettier for one thing.

JELLIED WATERCRESS SOUP
(For four)

1 can jellied chicken consommé
1 tablespoon lemon juice
1 cup of watercress leaves
chopped chives
1 hard-cooked egg

Take ¹/₂ the jellied consommé and put in the blender with the leaves of the watercress. Blend. Add rest of consommé and lemon juice. Serve jellied, with chopped chives and grated hard-cooked egg white.

ESSENCE OF CELERY SOUP
(For four or six)

3 cans chicken consommé
2 sprigs parsley
¹/₂ bay leaf
1 whole clove
1 egg
¹/₂ cup slivered celery
1 leek sliced thin, white part only

Simmer at low heat the consommé, parsley, bay leaf and clove for 1 hour. Break an egg, shell and all, into mixture. Bring to a rapid boil and strain. Add celery and leeks and cook 1 minute. Lazy? Just add celery and leeks to canned consommé and heat.

MOLDED FRUIT SALAD
(For four or six)

1 tablespoon gelatin
2 tablespoons cold water
$1/4$ cup boiling water
$1^1/_2$ cups dietetic ginger ale
1 tablespoon lemon juice
1 tablespoon grated orange or lemon peel
2 cups fresh or canned mixed fruit
No fresh pineapple, or you'll have no molded
   salad.

Soak gelatin in cold water. Add boiling water. Cool, add ginger ale, lemon juice and the peel. As it begins to congeal, fold in fruit. Pour in individual molds or a ring. Refrigerate overnight. Serve with whipped cottage cheese (skim milk) and grated orange peel for dressing.

PINEAPPLE CHEESE SALAD
(For four)

1 tablespoon gelatin
$1/4$ cup cold water
2 cups unsweetened pineapple juice
1 cup diced water-packed pineapple
2 tablespoons lemon juice
$1/2$ cup dry cottage cheese
2 tablespoons grated carrot

Dissolve gelatin in cold water. Melt over hot water. Add pineapple juice. When it begins to congeal, add rest of ingredients and mold in a ring. Refrigerate until firm. Unmold on greens and fill center with curls of carrot, celery and sliced radishes. Pass yogurt dressing with poppyseed sprinkled in it.

RED HOT JELLY

1 cup water
2 teaspoons Tabasco sauce
1$^{1}/_{2}$ teaspoons gelatin
$^{1}/_{3}$ cup lemon juice
artificial sweetener
red food coloring

Boil water and add to gelatin dissolved in the Tabasco sauce. Cool and add lemon juice, artificial sweetener and food coloring. Pour into a shallow pan to congeal. Cut in small cubes and mix with salad greens. Nice to serve when the entrée is beef.

RAW STUFFED MUSHROOMS
(For four)

8 raw mushrooms
$^{1}/_{2}$ cup cottage cheese
1 tablespoon skim milk
1 teaspoon chopped chives
few drops Worcestershire sauce

Wash and peel mushrooms. Remove stems (keep, chop and boil to add to vegetables in place of butter). Whip the cheese with the milk and add rest of ingredients. Stuff each mushroom cap and chill. These are nice to pass with a before-dinner drink.

TOMATO AND EGGPLANT PIE
(For four or six)

1 teaspoon Parmesan cheese
1 small eggplant peeled, sliced and steamed
2 peeled tomatoes sliced
1 green pepper, seeded and sliced
$^{1}/_{2}$ clove garlic chopped fine
1 tablespoon salad oil
2 teaspoons Parmesan cheese

Sprinkle Parmesan cheese in oven-proof pie casserole. Add eggplant, tomatoes and peppers. Sprinkle garlic, oil and rest of cheese over. Bake at 350° for 40 minutes.

ARTICHOKE SOUFFLÉ
(For four or six)

2 tablespoons whipped margarine
2 tablespoons flour
$^1/_2$ cup skim milk
1 teaspoon grated onion
4 egg yolks, beaten
2 cups mashed canned artichoke bottoms
5 egg whites

Melt margarine, add flour, cook until bubbly. Add milk, cook until thick. Add onion, and season with salt substitute and white pepper. Add yolks and mashed artichokes. Let mixture get cold. Fold in egg whites beaten stiff. Pour into lightly greased ring mold. Set in pan of hot water. Bake at 350° for 45 minutes. Let stand 10 minutes before unmolding. Use same recipe for broccoli.

MEXICAN SLAW SALAD
(For four)

1 package lemon Jello or D-Zerta
$1^1/_2$ cups hot water
$^1/_4$ cup vinegar
$^1/_4$ cup finely chopped celery
$^1/_2$ cup finely shredded cabbage
$^1/_4$ cup finely cut green pepper
2 tablespoons chopped sweet red pepper or pimiento

Pour the hot water over the Jello. When completely melted, add vinegar. Cool. When partially congealed, add rest of ingredients for a fresh crisp-tasting salad. If you add the vegetables while mixture is warm, they

77

are limp. Pour in mold. Refrigerate until firm. Unmold on salad greens. Serve with yogurt dressing.

GARDEN SOUP

This was served to me in Cuernavaca, Mexico. I had a house there for a vacation and balked at the high-calorie three meals a day routine. My cook came up with this.

(For two)

1 can chicken consommé
$1/4$ cup chopped raw spinach
$1/4$ cup watercress leaves
1 tablespoon chopped chives
2 green onions, sliced, green and white parts
2 eggs

Bring consommé to a boil. Add vegetables and simmer for 5 minutes. Drop eggs in and let poach. Season to your taste. Serve at once.

I liked it, and asked for it again. The next time I sprinkled Parmesan cheese over it.

DIPS

Whip cottage cheese with skim milk until consistency of whipped cream. Add herbs or chopped clams or curry or horseradish. Or carefully stir in caviar, with or without the horseradish. Or chop up very fine whatever raw vegetables you have and add. Add melted gelatin to any of this mixture and mold. You can balance your slice on a slice of cucumber while the rest indulge in crackers or melba toast.

By the way, I said to make your own melba toast. Buy a loaf of the best unsliced bread you can find and refrigerate until you can slice easily. Slice paper-thin, put on a cookie tray in a cold oven and turn to 200°. Leave until dry and light brown, or put in a dying oven and leave until you need it. The melba toast at The

Greenhouse is so thin a guest suggested serving it with solid-gold tweezers to pick it up with. Your toast, too, should be that thin.

CELERY HEARTS VINAIGRETTE
(For four)

4 canned celery hearts or freshly boiled pieces of celery
1 tablespoon tarragon vinegar
2 tablespoons cider vinegar
4 tablespoons salad oil
1 tablespoon chopped cucumber pickle
1 teaspoon chopped parsley
1 teaspoon chopped chives

Mix and serve over celery, with or without a bed of greens. Use it over hot vegetables also. Any kind.

BOUILLABAISSE SALAD
(For four)

2 heads Boston lettuce
1 bunch watercress
1 cup fresh or canned crabmeat
1 lobster tail, cooked and sliced
1 pound cooked shrimp
$1/2$ cup slivered celery
1 hard-cooked egg, chopped
1 tablespoon chopped chives
1 small sweet onion thinly sliced. You may omit.
2 peeled tomatoes quartered

Break lettuce into a bowl and add watercress leaves. Arrange the seafood in an attractive manner on top of the greens. Pour boiling water over the celery, drain and add, with the chopped egg and chives. Place tomatoes around the edge. Pile the onions on top. Bring to the table and pour on this dressing that has been put in a blender.

79

$^1/_2$ cup red wine vinegar
4 tablespoons salad oil
2 tablespoons Vermouth
$^1/_2$ teaspoon dry mustard
$^1/_2$ teaspoon paprika
1 teaspoon salt substitute

Sprinkle caviar on if you feel extravagant, and toss.

Artichokes of all kinds are low in calories and, for
the most part, everyone likes them. Whole hot fresh
ones make an elegant first course with mustard sauce
to dip the leaves in; use as a cold vegetable with Vinaigrette sauce, or as a luncheon salad, for example.
Have guests when you have this!

ARTICHOKES STUFFED WITH SHRIMP
AND HEARTS OF PALM
(For four)

4 artichokes
1 tablespoon lemon juice
2 teaspoons salt substitute

Trim stem of each artichoke. Pull off tough leaves at
base. Cut off top third and spread each artichoke open.
Dig out center fuzzy portion with a spoon or grapefruit
knife. Place in a deep saucepan. Add boiling water,
lemon juice and salt substitute to cover. Cover and
cook 30 minutes or until a leaf pulls out easily. Remove and drain. Place in a bowl to fit snugly and
pour $^1/_2$ cup wine vinegar dressing over. Marinate for
several hours or overnight. In the meantime prepare
filling:

1 cup sliced cooked shrimp
$^1/_2$ cup sliced hearts of palm or celery
1 tablespoon grated orange peel
8 whole cooked shrimp

Mix sliced shrimp, hearts of palm and grated orange peel. Remove artichokes from marinade and fill with the mixture. Decorate with the whole shrimp and chill. Pass yogurt dressing.

TOMATOES

Tomatoes are a good diet vegetable and there are ways to make them more enjoyable. Sprinkle them with Parmesan cheese or oregano or a little of both before baking. Cut in quarters and sprinkle with curry before baking or broiling. Cover with chopped shallots and mushrooms (a good way to use up the stems). Rub with mustard or catsup before broiling. Sprinkle chives over them as heavily as you wish, to serve either hot or cold.

ENDIVE

Endive sounds like and is an expensive fresh vegetable. You can buy it in cans also. Either way, place in a shallow casserole and cover with beef consommé. Sprinkle with chives or minced shallots and bake until soft and the consomme is evaporated. If fresh, season with salt substitute and white pepper.

SQUASH

Many men tell me they dislike squash. That is before they try it. Both men and women have preconceived ideas of what they like, and of course pass them down to their children. Someone really did a good job on squash. Little yellow squash cooked just tender, then split and covered with coarsely grated lemon peel and chopped pimiento, then put back in the oven to heat, is good — they like! Also add a little chopped cooked onion. But as you cook every vegetable, watch and don't overcook.

NUTS

I have listed nuts as high-calorie, but a few pine nuts in salad (by few, I mean, few, like 4 or 5 for you) sprinkled over cooked cabbage makes it divinely interesting.

ROAST CHICKEN FILLED WITH GRAPES
(For four)

1 4-pound roasting chicken
1 tablespoon lemon juice
1 teaspoon salt substitute
1 teaspoon paprika
white, red or blue fresh grapes
1 cup dry Sauternes wine or water

Wash and dry chicken. Rub with lemon juice and seasonings. Stuff cavity full with grapes left whole. Roast at 300°, basting several times with the wine and drippings. Bring to table whole and carve, serving grapes with the chicken. Pass pan juices with any fat skimmed off.

ROAST LOIN OR RACK OF VEAL
(For four)

1 2^1/$_2$-pound veal loin or rack (it should be white veal if possible)
^{1}/$_2$ teaspoon white pepper
^{1}/$_8$ teaspoon cinnamon
pinch of nutmeg
^{1}/$_2$ cup water or dry white wine
grated rind of 1 lemon
juice of 1 lemon

If using a veal loin, have the butcher bone, roll and tie for you. Rub with pepper, cinnamon and nutmeg. Place in pan in a 250° oven. After 1 hour add rind and juice. Baste with wine or water. Roast for

2 hours or until fork thrust into meat comes out easily. Serve with juices.

BROILED SQUAB

Have the poultry man split the squab open like a butterfly. Rub with salt substitute and white pepper. Broil breast side down for 8 minutes. Turn and broil 10 minutes more. The oven rack should be at least 8 inches from the heat. Do not overcook. Serve with ¹/₂ lemon. You work hard to eat a squab and if it were I, I'd use my fingers.

MEAT BALLS IN CONSOMMÉ
(For four)

1 small hard roll
¹/₂ pound ground beef
¹/₂ pound ground veal
2 tablespoons grated onion
¹/₂ teaspoon grated lemon peel
3 eggs beaten
1 tablespoon lemon juice
1 teaspoon salt substitute
¹/₂ teaspoon Worcestershire Sauce

The butcher will mix the meat for you. Moisten roll with water. Squeeze all the water out. Add rest of ingredients and mix thoroughly. Add a little chopped parsley if you wish. Shape into 8 balls and drop into hot consommé. Cover and simmer for 15 minutes. Serve in a shallow casserole with the consommé and chopped parsley.

You could buy frozen meat balls and then go on from there. They are not as good.

MIXED GRILL

In cooking calf's liver, be sure you have the real thing.   83

Have it sliced thin, and allow 1 ounce for you. Sauté quickly in a Teflon skillet, or broil. Do it quickly and don't overcook. Sprinkle with salt substitute and white pepper and, if you choose, a little claret wine, before cooking. The kidney, $1/2$ for you, should be sliced thin and treated the same way; and all the fat should be trimmed from the lamb chop.

POACHED RED SNAPPER
(For four)

4 6-ounce portions boned and skinned red snapper
2 cups water
1 lemon sliced
1 small onion sliced
3 peppercorns
2 sprigs parsley
1 bay leaf

Place fish in skillet and cover with rest of ingredients. Cover and simmer for 5 to 8 minutes or until fish will flake easily when tested with a fork. Remove fish to hot platter. Serve with

EGG SAUCE

2 tablespoons whipped margarine
1 tablespoon flour
$1/2$ teaspoon dry mustard
$1/2$ cup skim milk plus $1/2$ cup poaching liquid
2 hard-cooked egg whites, chopped
1 tablespoon chopped parsley

Melt margarine, add flour and mustard. Cook till bubbly and add milk and poaching liquid. Cook until thickened. Add egg whites and parsley. Pour over fish.

You may poach in dry white wine or half wine, half water. Or steam your fish in your steamette — you must have one by now.

BARBECUED CHICKEN
(For four)

2 1½-pound broiling chickens, split
2 teaspoons Vegesalt
4 teaspoons Worcestershire Sauce
2 bay leaves
½ cup vinegar
1 cup water or wine
1 cup tomato juice
½ teaspoon dry mustard
2 cloves garlic finely chopped
½ teaspoon paprika
¼ teaspoon cayenne pepper
1 teaspoon sugar substitute

Wash and dry broiling chickens. Mix rest of ingredients in a saucepan and cook for 10 minutes. Place chickens on broiling rack breast side down, and spoon some of the sauce over. Broil for 10 minutes. Turn and baste with sauce, continuing to cook for about 45 minutes, or until chicken is tender. Or broil out of doors over charcoal and baste frequently. Use the same recipe for barbecued red snapper.

DEVILED EGGS WITH CAVIAR
(For four)

4 hard-cooked eggs
¼ teaspoon prepared mustard
1 tablespoon skim milk
1 tablespoon vinegar
1 teaspoon chopped parsley
½ teaspoon salt substitute
⅛ teaspoon white pepper
red or black caviar

Split eggs in half, remove yolks and mash. Add mustard, milk, vinegar, parsley and seasonings. Whip with a fork until light. Pile in the white halves and spoon caviar on top.

BAKED PEARS WITH LEMON SAUCE
(For four)

4 fresh pears
1/2 cup water
3 cloves
1 teaspoon artificial sweetener

Place pears in casserole. Add water, cloves and artificial sweetener. Cover and bake at 350° until tender. Serve hot with cold lemon sauce.

LEMON SAUCE

1 tablespoon cornstarch
1 cup boiling water
2 teaspoons grated lemon peel
2 tablespoons lemon juice
1/2 teaspoon artificial sweetener
a few drops of yellow vegetable coloring

Dissolve cornstarch in a little cold water. Add hot water and cook until clear. Cool and add juice and lemon peel and sweetener.

WINE JELLY PARFAIT
(For four)

1 tablespoon gelatin
1 tablespoon lemon juice
1/3 cup orange juice
1/2 cup hot water
3/4 cup orange juice
1/2 cup port wine
grated rind of orange
sugar substitute

Sprinkle gelatin over first-listed juices and dissolve. Add hot water. When cold, add orange juice, port wine and grated orange peel. When set, spoon into parfait glasses, and decorate with fresh fruit if you like.

ORANGE SHERBET

3 cups fresh orange juice
2 tablespoons lemon juice
1 cup non-fat dried milk
grated rind of 1 orange
sweetening to your taste

Mix and freeze in crank freezer. Or put in ice trays. Remove when solid and beat. Return to freeze again.

BAKED APPLE

You really do not bake an apple. Core, and peel halfway down. Add peelings to water — use 1/4 cup water for each apple — and boil for flavor and color. Add sweetener to your taste. Add apples and poach till tender. Remove, strain juices and pour over apples. Run under broiler to brown.

STEAMED FRUIT

The flavor and texture of fresh steamed fruit is delightful. Use your steamette. Peel fruit like peaches, pears, apricots and apples. Place in the steamette, rub with sweetener, place over hot water, cover and steam about 4 or 5 minutes. Serve hot or cold.

LEMON ICE CREAM

This is a refreshing dessert and you can combine it with fresh fruits to make a beautiful dessert. I think it needs special crystal, like a brandy snifter or champagne glass to carry it, and a green leaf or flower at the base.

1 quart plus 1³/₄ cups skim milk
³/₄ cup lemon juice
2 teaspoons grated lemon peel
a few drops yellow vegetable coloring
artificial sweetener to your taste

Mix and freeze in a freezer.

FLOATING ISLAND

2 egg yolks
2 cups scalded skim milk
artificial sweetener
¹/₂ teaspoon lemon extract
1 teaspoon grated lemon peel
2 egg whites
artificial sweetener

Beat egg yolks, add scalded milk and cook over hot water until thickened. Sweeten and add flavoring and lemon peel. Cool. When ready to serve, pour into a large crystal bowl. Beat egg whites with sweetener to soft peaks. Drop into bowl by spoonfuls. Sprinkle with more lemon peel if you wish.

SPECIAL OCCASIONS

A BUFFET DINNER

Roasted Leg of Veal, Natural Gravy
Celery, Mushrooms and Snow Peas
Molded Spinach Ring
Cold Boiled Lobster Tail in Shells
Sliced Cucumbers in Yogurt
Help Yourself Salad Tray with Green Herb Dressing
Pear Halves filled with Whipped Cottage Cheese
  (you add skim milk before whipping) with
Puréed Raspberries spilled over
A suggested wine: Givry, Pinot Noir de Bourgogne   89

ROAST LEG OF VEAL
(For eight or ten)

1 6-to-8-pound round of veal (bone in is always better for flavor)
1 teaspoon paprika
1 teaspoon each of tarragon, rosemary and oregano
1 tablespoon salt substitute
2 tablespoons chopped parsley
2 tablespoons chopped shallots or onion
1 cup red wine
1 cup water or consommé
1 can artichoke hearts

Rub veal with the seasonings mixed together. Place in a roasting pan and add the parsley and shallots. Roast at 325° for about 3 hours. Baste frequently with the wine and water. Remove meat from pan, skim off any fat. Slice the artichokes and add to juices if you like, otherwise serve without thickening.

MOLDED SPINACH RING
(For eight or ten)

3 pounds fresh spinach
1/4 cup chopped onion
2 tablespoons chopped chives
salt substitute
pepper
a few grains grated nutmeg

Wash spinach thoroughly, drain and put in a pot with the water that clings to the leaves, and the onion. Cook covered for 5 minutes. Turn into a colander and drain, then into a blender and make a purée. Add chives and seasonings. Put into a lightly greased ring

90

mold. Set in a pan of water to heat. Turn out on a
hot tray and sprinkle with grated carrots.

HELP YOURSELF SALAD TRAY

This is an especially good idea to serve on any buffet.
For one thing, you can clean out your icebox and
pantry. A selection of individual tomato aspics, canned
whole tiny green beans garnished with thin slices of
red onion, canned white or green asparagus garnished
with slices of hard-cooked egg whites and chopped
pimiento, pickled beets — you name it — but arrange
it attractively for guests to make their choice.

GREEN HERB DRESSING

$^1/_2$ cup parsley leaves
$^1/_2$ cup watercress leaves
8 peeled shallots or scallions
2 teaspoons dry mustard
1 teaspoon horseradish
1 teaspoon Worcestershire
2 egg yolks
1 cup salad oil
$^1/_3$ cup tarragon vinegar
1 teaspoon mixed dried herbs

Put in a blender and whip until thickened. Thin with
cold water and dribble over greens.

OPEN HOUSE OR COCKTAIL PARTY

I have heard so many of my friends bewail the high-
calorie pick-ups usually served at a party. If you keep
your party fare lower in calories, you can at least have
a clear conscience when your guests go on somewhere
else for dinner. 91

THE MENU

Gazpacho in a punch bowl or soup tureen with a block of floating ice to keep it cold

A tray of chopped cucumbers, tomatoes, chives and celery made more substantial by the attractive containers

Windmill Phosphates (ice water) in silver pitchers with stemmed glasses to drink from. You may as well get used to these and order them at a sophisticated cocktail lounge. I did at New York's famed "21." What fun!

Hot boiled shrimp in beer, mustard dressing to dip them in

Hot meat balls sautéed with shallots and Burgundy wine

Hot Chicken Teriyaki

Marinated artichoke hearts in mint dressing

Fresh raw mushrooms filled with caviar

Cherry tomatoes filled with cottage cheese whipped up with chives and Worcestershire sauce

Small cooked cold zucchini sprinkled with anise seeds and red wine vinegar

Hard-boiled egg white halves filled with Salmon Mousse

A high compote filled with melon balls

Demitasse

RECIPES

CHICKEN TERIYAKI
(For twelve)

6 5-ounce chicken breasts
2 tablespoons sherry wine
1 clove garlic
$^1/_2$ cup soy sauce
$^1/_2$ teaspoon sugar substitute

Skin chicken and cut in 1-inch pieces. Cover with rest
of ingredients and refrigerate for a minimum of 3 hours.
Put two or three pieces on bamboo skewers. Broil
5 minutes, turning once.

BOILED SHRIMP IN BEER
(For twelve)

4 pounds large shrimp, peeled and cleaned
2 cloves garlic, crushed
2 pieces celery
few sprigs parsley
2 quarts beer

Put shrimp with garlic, celery and parsley in boiling
beer, and cook covered for 5 minutes. Drain. Serve
in a casserole with a little of the liquid to keep warm,
and picks to spear with.

SALMON MOUSSE

12 eggs
2 tablespoons lemon juice
$1/2$ cup finely chopped celery
$1/4$ cup finely chopped pickle
1 tablespoon grated onion
2 cups canned salmon, drained and flaked
2 teaspoons horseradish
1 cup skim milk
1 teaspoon gelatin

Hard-cook the eggs and remove the yolks. Mix all the
ingredients to a smooth paste, except the gelatin.
Dissolve the gelatin in a little of the juice from the
salmon and melt over hot water. Add to salmon mixture and fill the egg cavities with it. Garnish with some
of the egg yolks grated and mixed with chopped
parsley. Refrigerate.   93

BACK YARD WHING-DING

Colored cloths, gay flowers, artificial or fresh, yard candles and noise can be distracting for you, but make your guests enjoy the lower-in-calorie supper.

Pitchers of Sangria for each table
Your old wheelbarrow freshly and gaily spray-painted (outside) filled with ice and raw vegetables, i.e., scallions, raw mushrooms, carrot and turnip sticks, radishes and whatever else you may choose
Charcoal-broiled Flank Steak, carved at the broiler
Zucchini Squash and Tomato Casserole
My Favorite Cole Slaw
Pickled Beets and Onions
Fresh Strawberry Ice with
Fresh Strawberries to nibble

RECIPES

SANGRIA

Juice of 1 lemon
Juice of 1 orange
Juice of 1 lime
1 cinnamon stick
1 cup water
1 teaspoon sugar substitute
1 bottle Red Burgundy wine

Bring juices, cinnamon stick and water to a boil. Add sugar substitute and check for taste. Cool, add wine. Put in pitchers with sliced fresh fruit, such as peaches, fresh pineapple, cherries, apricots. Refrigerate several hours. Serve with fruit.

ZUCCHINI AND TOMATOES
(For eight or ten)

6 zucchini
2 peeled and sliced tomatoes
1/4 cup finely chopped onion
2 tablespoons finely chopped parsley
1 tablespoon salad oil
salt substitute
white pepper
1 tablespoon Parmesan cheese

Parboil zucchini until tender crisp. Slice in 1/4-inch slices. Place in alternate layers with tomato and onion in shallow casserole. Sprinkle with oil and seasonings. Sprinkle with cheese. Bake at 325° for 15 minutes or until casserole is sizzling hot and cheese is brown.

STRAWBERRY ICE

2 quarts fresh strawberries
1 cup honey
2 cups cold water
2 tablespoons lemon juice
artificial sweetener to taste

Pour honey over hulled and washed berries. Mash and let stand for 30 minutes. Put in a blender or force through a sieve. Add water and lemon juice. Freeze.

Keeping slim can be a family affair. Teen-agers have weight problems too and should be encouraged to maintain a routine that will help them get ready for adult life.

Coke parties can be as much fun with a fruit cooler and better for all. A back yard party with tiny frankfurters and small hamburgers for guests to cook themselves will keep them busy, and trays of raw vegetables and fruit will make them forget the usual routine.

FRUIT COOLER
(For one)

Juice of 1 orange
Juice of ½ lemon
Ice Water
Artificial sweetener
Chunks of whatever fresh fruit is available
Homemade fresh fruit ice
Paper umbrellas

Sweeten juices and water with artificial sweetener. Put in tall glass with fruit, and fill with more water if needed. Float a scoop of ice on top, and stick a little paper umbrella in it, and a sprig of mint if any is around.

SOUTH OF THE BORDER PARTY

Molded Beef Consommé with Slivers of Avocado and Leeks
Chili and Enchiladas
Green Peppers filled with Marinated Vegetables and Tuna
Green Salad with thin slices of Red Sweet Pepper and Red Onions
Tangerines flamed with Brandy
Tray of Fresh Pineapple Sticks and Slices of Sharp Cheese

RECIPES

AVOCADO AND LEEK MOLD
(For eight or ten)

3 cans beef consommé
1 ripe avocado
2 bunches leeks, boiled and sliced

Melt consommé if jelled, if not, add 1 teaspoon of gelatin for each cup and heat. Pour half into a ring mold and add very thin slices of avocado. When this has congealed, add leeks to other half and pour on top. Refrigerate overnight. Unmold on salad greens.

LOW-CALORIE CHILI
(For eight or ten)

2¹/₂ pounds lean coarse-ground beef
2 tablespoons chili powder
¹/₄ cup diced chili pods, stems and seeds removed
1 cup canned tomatoes, mashed
¹/₂ cup chopped onion
1 garlic bud chopped fine
1 quart water

Cook meat in a heavy saucepan until brown. Add chili powder, garlic, tomatoes and cook 10 minutes. Add onions and cook 10 minutes longer. Add the chili pods to the water and boil until soft. Add to rest of ingredients and cook slowly for 20 minutes. Add more water if necessary.

You could roll this mixture up in cabbage leaves wilted in hot water, sprinkle with Parmesan cheese and bake for a lower-in-calorie version of an enchilada.

STUFFED GREEN PEPPERS
(For twelve)

12 medium-sized green peppers
1 cup fresh-cooked green beans or tiny canned
    ones
1 cup cooked asparagus, cut in pieces
2 cups diced fresh tomatoes
2 cans water-packed tuna, flaked
1 cup garlic dressing

Toss the vegetables and tuna fish with the garlic dressing. Cut off the tops of the peppers, remove seeds and scallop the edges. Stuff vegetables into pepper shells. Garnish with pimiento.

A POKER PARTY FOR THE MAN ABOUT THE HOUSE

A Chafing Dish of Onion Soup
Roasted Peppered Rib Eye of Beef
Thick Slices of Tomato sprinkled with No-Calorie
    Dressing and Dill
Cottage Cheese and Horseradish Mousse
Raw Vegetable Sticks
Raisin Clusters
Coffee or Sanka

Put a red felt cloth on the table and decorate it with some substantial pottery and a pot of red geraniums. The men will feel better the next day.

Onion Soup can be as low-calorie as you like. Merely boil thinly sliced yellow onions until soft. Add to canned chicken and canned beef consommé, half and half. Sprinkle with Parmesan cheese as served.

PEPPERED RIB EYE OF BEEF
(For twelve or fourteen)

1 6-8 pound rib eye of beef, stripped of all fat
2 tablespoons salad oil
$1/4$ or $1/2$ can cracked or fresh ground pepper
$1/2$ cup red Burgundy wine
1 onion
1 carrot
1 piece celery
Vegesalt

Rub beef with oil, Vegesalt and pepper, the amount depending on your taste. I like it heavily peppered. Place in a shallow pan with the onion, carrot and celery. Roast uncovered at 350° — 15 minutes for each pound or more, depending on how well cooked you like it. Baste frequently with the wine and consommé if you need more liquid. Serve with strained pan juices.

COTTAGE CHEESE
AND HORSERADISH MOUSSE
(For four)

1 cup skimmed milk cottage cheese
$1/4$ cup skimmed milk
2 tablespoons horseradish (sauce or fresh
    grated)
2 tablespoons vinegar

Put into a blender and whip to the consistency of whipped cream. Melt 1 teaspoon gelatin in a little cold water and add. Pour into a mold and refrigerate. No one will believe it low calorie, and think what variations you can have!

ASPIC RINGS

Jellied consommé cut with a round cutter, piled with caviar.

ROAST CAPON WITH TRUFFLE SAUCE
(For eight)

1 5-to-6-pound capon
1 apple
1 orange
1 onion
$1/8$ teaspoon cinnamon
1 tablespoon salt substitute
1 cup dry white wine or water
1 truffle

Wash and dry capon. Fill cavity with apple, orange and onion. Rub capon with cinnamon and salt substitute. Put in a 325° oven and baste with the wine. Roast for 3 hours or until capon is done. The leg bone will "wiggle" when you test it. Remove, skim fat off drippings and add thin slices of black truffle to the sauce.

CRANBERRY HORSERADISH MOUSSE
(For eight or ten)

2 cups cranberries
$1/2$ cup water
1 teaspoon sugar substitute
2 teaspoons gelatin

Wash berries, add water and boil for 5 minutes. Put in blender. Sweeten to your taste. Add gelatin while hot.

1 cup cottage cheese
2 tablespoons skim milk
2 tablespoons horseradish

Mash cheese with milk, add horseradish and whip until light and fluffy. Combine with the cranberry mixture and pour into star-shape mold. Refrigerate overnight. Unmold on bleached endive for a pretty relish for capon or turkey.

EGGNOG ICE CREAM

1 quart skim milk
1 tablespoon cornstarch
3 egg yolks, beaten
1 teaspoon vanilla
1/4 cup Bourbon
artificial sweetener

Scald 3 1/2 cups of the milk. Mix the cornstarch with the rest. Add to the milk and cook until thickened. Add egg yolks. Cook 1 minute. Cool. Add vanilla. Heat Bourbon and ignite. When flame has died, add to custard. Sweeten to your taste and freeze.

By now you know you can have a variety of meals low in calories, and you can find other ways yourself. If you are your own cook, you may have found even better ways. If you have a cook, she no doubt needed the diet too and cooperated. Just accept the fact that you have to diet. You may splurge once in a while, but get back in the swing again.

I do — you can.

Index

INDEX

112

113